# TRADITIONS AND CELEBRATIONS

# EARTH DAY

by Melissa Ferguson

PEBBLE
a capstone imprint

Pebble Explore is published by Pebble, an imprint of Capstone.
1710 Roe Crest Drive
North Mankato, Minnesota 56003
www.capstonepub.com

**Library of Congress Cataloging-in-Publication Data**
Names: Ferguson, Melissa, author.
Title: Earth Day / by Melissa Ferguson.
Description: North Mankato, Minnesota : Pebble 2021. | Series: Pebble explore. Traditions and celebrations | Includes bibliographical references and index. | Audience: Ages 6-8 | Audience: Grades 2-3 |
Summary: "Earth Day celebrates our beautiful planet and calls us to act on its behalf. Some people spend the day planting flowers or trees. Others organize neighborhood clean-ups, go on nature walks, or make recycled crafts. Readers will discover how a shared holiday can have multiple traditions and be celebrated in all sorts of ways"-- Provided by publisher.
Identifiers: LCCN 2020038001 (print) | LCCN 2020038002 (ebook) | ISBN 9781977131867 (hardcover) | ISBN 9781977132888 (paperback) | ISBN 9781977154132 (pdf) | ISBN 9781977155849 (kindle edition)
Subjects: LCSH: Earth Day--Juvenile literature. | Environmentalism--Juvenile literature. Classification: LCC GE195.5 .F47 2021 (print) | LCC GE195.5 (ebook) | DDC 394.262--dc23 LC record available at https://lccn.loc.gov/2020038001 LC ebook record available at https://lccn.loc.gov/2020038002

**Image Credits**
Alamy: ClassicStock/H. Armstrong Roberts, 7, Michael Wheatley, 11; Getty/SOPA Images, 8; iStockphoto: Johnce, 29, Kenishirotie, 26, PeopleImages, 22, recep-bg, 18, SDI Productions, 24; Newscom: ENRIQUE CASTRO-MENDIVIL/REUTERS, 9, Jim West/ZUMA Press, 10; Shutterstock: amophoto_au, 23, David Pereiras, 19, frantic00, 1, FreeBird7977, 27, Janis Smits, 4, Monkey Business Images, 5, 25, New Africa, 28, Piyaphong25, 16, Rawpixel.com, 21, sarayut_sy, cover, SeventyFour, 15, sirikorn thamniyom, 14, vchal, 13, wavebreakmedia, 17

Artistic elements: Shutterstock/Rafal Kulik

**Editorial Credits**
Editor: Jill Kalz; Designer: Juliette Peters; Media Researcher: Kelly Garvin; Production Specialist: Spencer Rosio

# TABLE OF CONTENTS

Words in **bold** are in the glossary.

# OUR HOME

We all share one home. We share it with every plant and animal too. It's a big home! It's planet Earth.

Our surroundings on Earth are called the **environment**. Land, water, and air are all parts of it. A clean and safe environment is important for everyone.

# WHAT IS EARTH DAY?

Earth Day is a **celebration** of our planet. It happens every year on April 22.

The first Earth Day was in 1970. A man named Gaylord Nelson started it. He knew our environment needed to be **protected**. It gives us water, food, and the air we breathe. If those things aren't clean, the whole planet gets sick. Earth Day asks people around the world to take care of their home.

First Earth Day in 1970

Earth Day events take place around the world. People of all ages join in. Events happen in big cities and small towns. They happen in libraries and nature centers. They happen in schools and people's homes.

Helping the environment can seem like a huge job. It is! That's why everyone needs to help. Lots of small tasks add up to a big difference.

# PEOPLE AND TRADITIONS

Some people do the same things on Earth Day every year. **Traditions** make the day even more special. Anyone can start a tradition. Try starting one on Earth Day this year! There are lots of ideas in this book.

**Park cleanup day**

**Earth Day parade**

Cleanup days are a common tradition. People gather to clean parks and other places. They may also build bird or butterfly houses. Going to an Earth Day parade is another tradition. Parades are held in cities around the world.

# A TIME TO LEARN

Earth Day is a time to celebrate. It's also a time to learn. Lots of things harm our air, water, and land every day. **Pollution** is a big one. It makes things dirty.

Smoke from fires pollutes the air. Spilled oil pollutes oceans, rivers, and other bodies of water. Garbage pollutes the land. People can make a lot of pollution. But they can stop a lot of it too.

On Earth Day, some people go to the library. They learn about pollution and other dangers to our planet. They read books or news stories on the internet. They ask questions and try to find answers.

What things are hurting Earth?
Where do they come from? Can the
problems be fixed? How do we work
together? How do we keep our world
safe and healthy?

Some libraries have special Earth Day programs. Museums and nature centers may have them too. Speakers talk about the environment. They often show photos or videos. Speakers teach others how to care for the planet. Sometimes, seeds or tiny trees are given away for people to plant.

# CLEANUP DAYS

Many cities have cleanup days on Earth Day. People work with one another to clean the places where they live. They pick up garbage. They fix broken things. They mow grass and pull weeds. They plant trees or flowers.

Cleanup days are also held at beaches. Rivers and lakes have cleanup days too. Cleaning the land and water is important. It keeps people healthy. It also keeps animals and plants healthy.

# AT HOME

You can do many things at home to help Earth. Don't throw all of your garbage into one bin. Put paper, glass, and plastic items in their own bins. Most of these items can be **recycled**. Recycling helps keep garbage out of **landfills**.

Landfills are big. The garbage in them can make lots of pollution. That harms our air, water, and land. It harms all living things.

We use power to cook food and wash clothes. We use it to light our homes. We use power for cars, computers, and more. Making power can create pollution. Try to use less.

Turn off the lights when you leave a room. Keep your house cooler in winter and warmer in summer. Try to wear your clothes more than once before washing. Walk or bike to places, if you can. Leave the water off while you're brushing your teeth.

# AT SCHOOL

Kids celebrate Earth Day at school in lots of ways. Do you like to learn new things? Go to the library. Your teacher can help you find books or websites about Earth. Read about its many plants and animals. The more you know about Earth, the more you will want to protect it.

Do you like to tell stories? Write one about Earth Day. It can be true or made-up. Ask your teacher if you can share the story with your class.

Do you like art? Make posters for Earth Day. Show others what makes our planet great. Use markers or paints. Draw your favorite plants and animals. Draw the whole world! Add dried flowers, twigs, or shells.

Do you like playing in dirt? Some schools have gardens. See if you can help take care of it. Help plant seeds or pull weeds. Everyone can do something!

# EARTH DAY EVERY DAY

We celebrate Earth Day every year in April. But Earth Day shouldn't be just one day. It should be every day!

Keeping our planet clean and safe is a big, important job. You can help. Your friends and family can too. We all need the environment. And it needs all of us to take care of it. Let's keep Earth clean for years to come.

# GLOSSARY

**celebration** (sel-uh-BRAY-shuhn)—a special, happy gathering

**environment** (en-VY-ruhn-muhnt)—the natural world around us

**healthy** (HEL-thee)—being well, not sick

**landfill** (LAND-fill)—a place where garbage is buried

**pollution** (poh-LOO-shuhn)—materials that hurt Earth's air, water, and land

**protect** (proh-TEKT)—to keep safe

**recycle** (ree-SY-kuhl)—to turn used items into new ones

**tradition** (tra-DIH-shuhn)—a custom, idea, or belief passed down through time

# READ MORE

Grack, Rachel. *Earth Day*. Minneapolis: Bellwether Media, 2018.

Manley, Erika S. *Earth Day*. Minneapolis: Jump!, Inc., 2017.

McAnulty, Stacy. *Earth!: My First 4.54 Billion Years*. New York: Henry Holt and Company, 2017.

# INTERNET SITES

*Earth Day*
kids.nationalgeographic.com/explore/celebrations/earth-day/

*EEK! Environmental Education for Kids*
eekwi.org/

*Games, Quizzes, and Videos About the Environment*
epa.gov/students/games-quizzes-and-videos-about-environment

# INDEX